TH

LAUGH

Note from the publisher

This is a serious book about a humorous subject. Our aim is to portray some of the wonderful examples of witty or unusual epitaphs and quirky grave designs and to do so in a way that is both sensitive and respectful. We have no intention of causing any offence to relatives and friends of the deceased and sincerely hope that none is taken.

THE LAST
LAUGH

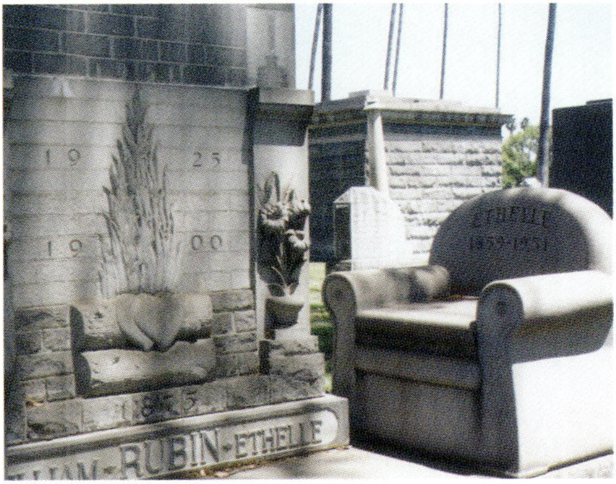

Marlin Press

Introduction

Amusing epitaphs and quirky grave designs have a poignancy and an impact that few other forms of humour manage to achieve. It is a rare brand of comedy, created by a small number of individuals with nothing in common other than a desire to raise a grin at their gravesides and to ensure that something of their personality lives on long after they are gone. The purpose of this book is to bring graveyard humour before a wider audience by illustrating some of the best examples – over 50 of the wittiest, cleverest, blackest, most outrageous things that people have had inscribed on, or designed into, their grave markers or memorial plaques.

Instances of graveyard humour can be found throughout hisory, and can say much about the times in which the deceased was laid to rest. Epitaphs like that for Ellen Shannon, "fatally burned Mar. 21, 1870, by the explosion of a lamp filled with R. Danforth's non explosive burning fluid" challenge our perception of the Victorian era as a time of excessive sobriety and reverence. More recent examples reflect contemporary themes or personal preoccupations, such as a grave shaped in the form of a CD player in Georgia, or a life-size granite replica of a Mercedes 240D in New Jersey.

Humorous graves usually occur as isolated examples amongst the rows of uniform headstones and conventional epitaphs in a cemetery, causing visitors or passers-by to smile, or with the most unusual or outlandish examples, to drop their jaws in disbelief. How often do you see a grave with the inscription "To the memory of our children, who sleep around"?

In some cases, one or more humorous graves are linked, either physically or by their epitaphs. A grave in Pennsylvania bears the inscription “Snuck as a bug”. Two rows along another grave has the epitaph “Snucker than that bugger over there”.

A very few graveyards make humour something of a speciality. Boot Hill Cemetery in Tombstone, Arizona, is a relic from the Old West, taking its name from the fact that so many of those interred there died violently, “with their boots on”. It fell to their judges or executioners to write their epitaphs along with their sentences, and they often did so in the blackest terms possible. Some examples are featured in this book.

On the other side of the Atlantic, at Sapinta in northern Romania, is the "Merry Cemetery", where all of the dead are remembered in a light-hearted way with depictions on their graves of their occupations and lifestyles, even the manner in which they died.

Humorous epitaphs are as varied as the personalities that devised them, and range from the terse one-liner to the potted autobiography. Some of the best lines comes from the professionals – comedians, writers, actors and directors – several of which are featured in this book. One of the most famous is the inscription on the grave of the comedian Spike Milligan – "I told you I was ill". Ironically, though he had requested this epitaph long before he died in 2002, his grave in Winchelsea, East Sussex, lay unmarked until 2004, and even then, the local diocese would allow it only if it was written in Gaelic.

Most of the photographs in this book have a caption that includes the inscription – for clarity – the location of the grave and where possible notes that explain the story behind the grave. For some of the examples featured the humour resides not in a funny line, but simply in the surname of the deceased, carved boldly in the stone; "Rich" and "Famous" are two examples. As the humour here is possibly unintentional, we have omitted the full names of the deceased and the locations of the graves, to preserve their anonymity.

For readers who are interested in exploring the genre further, there are several websites dedicated to recording examples, some of which are given in the photography credits on page 60. Alternatively, just enter "humorous graves" into your preferred search engine.

So, now for some last words of our own. We hope you enjoy this book and find its contents as amusing – and inspiring – as we did when putting it together. It takes a certain *chutzpah* to carve a joke in stone, one that will be associated with your name for eternity. But perhaps it says something about the indomitability of the human spirit. Death can take us from this world, but it cannot extinguish one of the things that makes us uniquely human – our sense of humour.

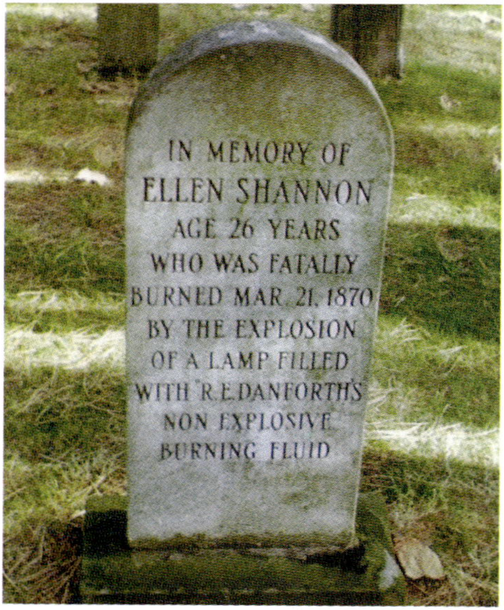

In memory of
Ellen Shannon
Age 26 years
Who was fatally
Burned Mar. 21, 1870
By the explosion
Of a lamp filled
With R. E. Danforth's
Non explosive
Burning Fluid

Church Street Cemetery, Girard, Pennsylvania

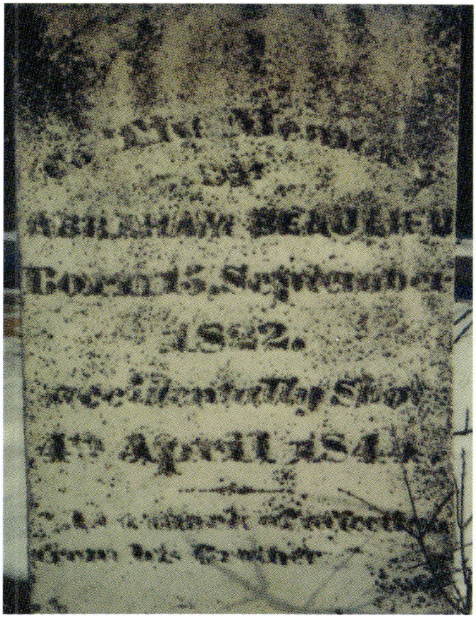

To the memory of
Abraham Beaulieu
Born 15 September
1822

Accidentally shot
4th April 1844
As a mark of affection
From his brother

Catholic Cemetery, La Pointe, Wisconsin

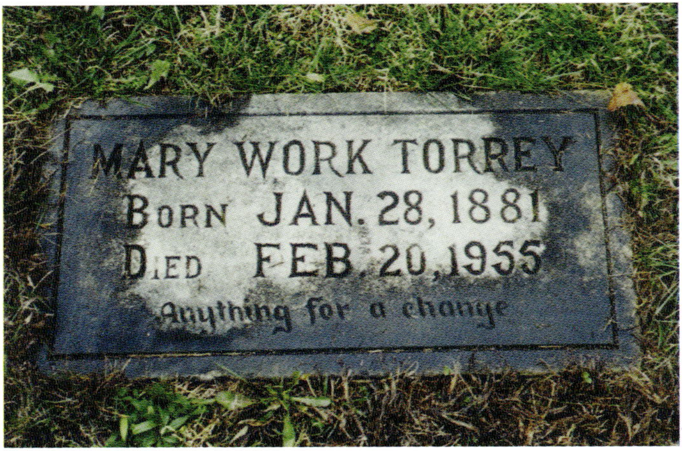

Mary Work Torrey
Born Jan. 28, 1881
Died Feb. 20, 1955

Anything for a change

New Gray Cemetery, Knoxville, Tennessee

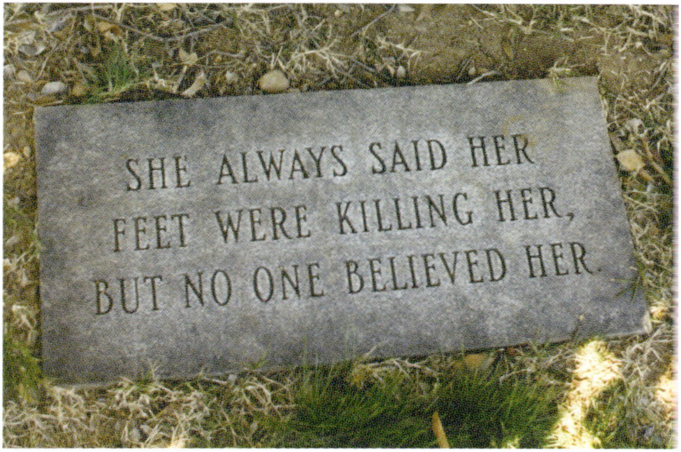

She always said her
Feet were killing her,
But no one believed her

Hollywood Cemetery, Richmond, Virginia

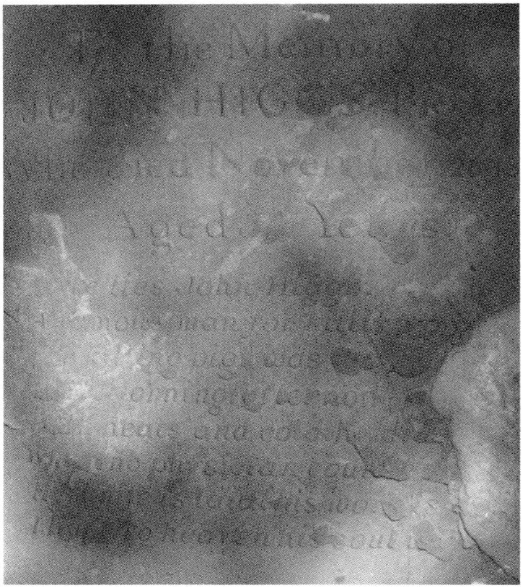

To the memory of John Higgs
Who died November 26 1825
Aged 34 years

Here lies John Higgs
A famous man for killing pigs,
For killing pigs was his delight
Both morning, afternoon and night;
Both heats and cold he did endure,
Which no physician could e'er cure;
His knife is laid, his work is done,
I hope to heaven his soul is gone.

St Mary's Church, Cheltenham, Gloucestershire

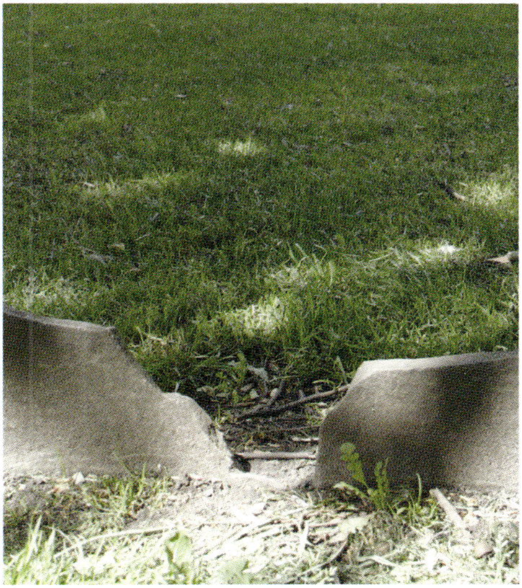

To the memory of John Paine, blacksmith, died 1796

My sledge and hammer lies reclined,
My bellows pipe have lost its wind,
My fire's extinct, my forge decayed,
And in the dust my vice is laid,
My coal is spent, my iron's gone,
My nails are drove, my work is done.

St Mary's Church, Cheltenham, Gloucestershire

(Only fragments of this grave remain; the inscription survives in the church records)

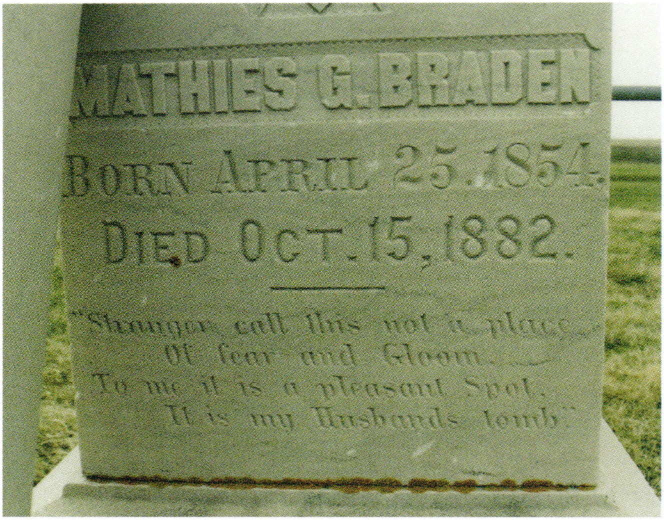

Mathies G. Braden
Born April 25, 1854.
Died Oct. 15, 1882.

"Stranger call this not a place
Of fear and gloom.
To me it is a pleasant spot.
It is my husband's tomb."

Old Mandan Cemetery, Near Bismarck, North Dakota

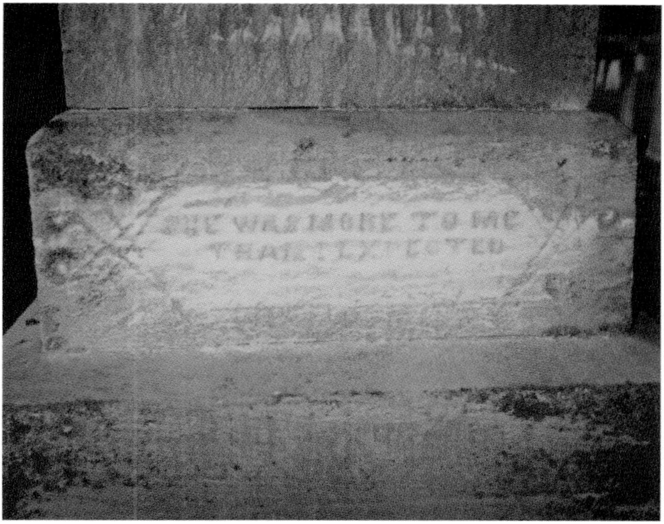

She was more to me
Than I expected

College Hill Cemetery, Lebanon, Illinois

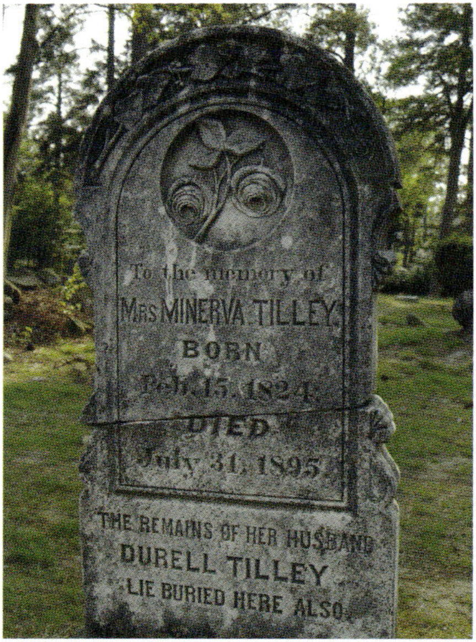

To the memory of
Mrs Minerva Tilley
Born
Feb. 15 1824;
Died
May 31 1895.

The remains of her husband
Durell Tilley
Lie buried here also

Old Chapel Hill Cemetery, Orange County, North Carolina

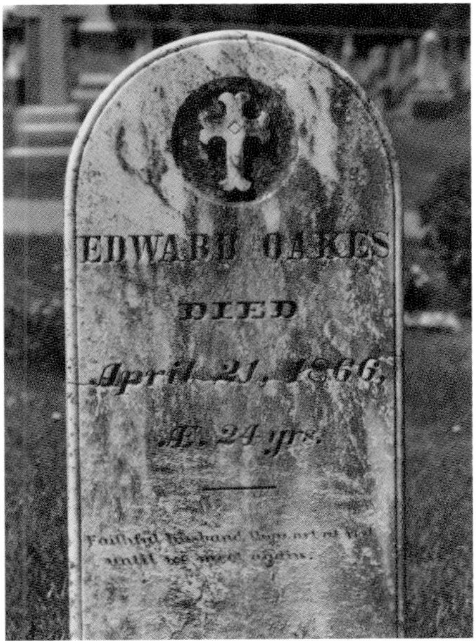

Edward Oakes
Died
April 21, 1866,
AE. 24 yrs.

Faithful husband thou are at rest
Until we meet again.

West Cemetery, Middlebury, Vermont

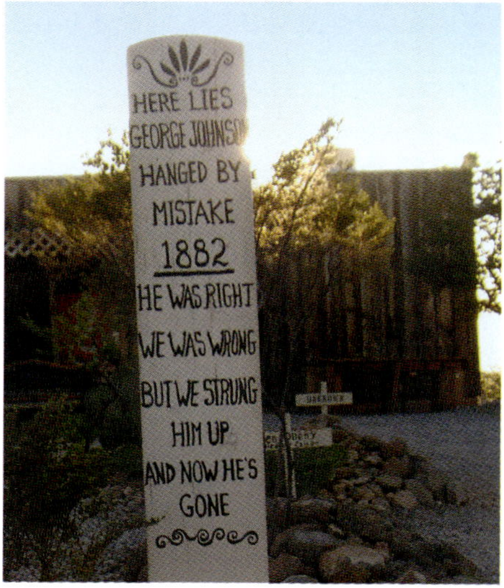

Here lies
George Johnson
Hanged by
Mistake
1882

He was right
We was wrong
But we strung
Him up
And now he's
Gone

Boot Hill Cemetery, Tombstone, Arizona

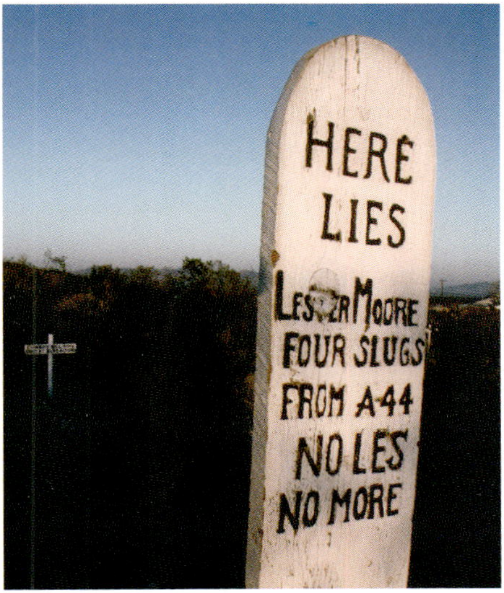

Here
lies
Lester Moore
Four Slugs
From a 44
No Les
No More

Boot Hill Cemetery, Tombstone, Arizona

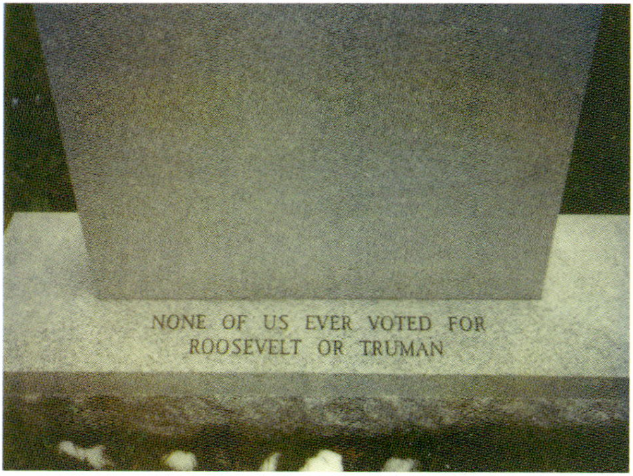

None of us ever voted for
Roosevelt or Truman

Elgin Cemetery, Elgin, Minnesota

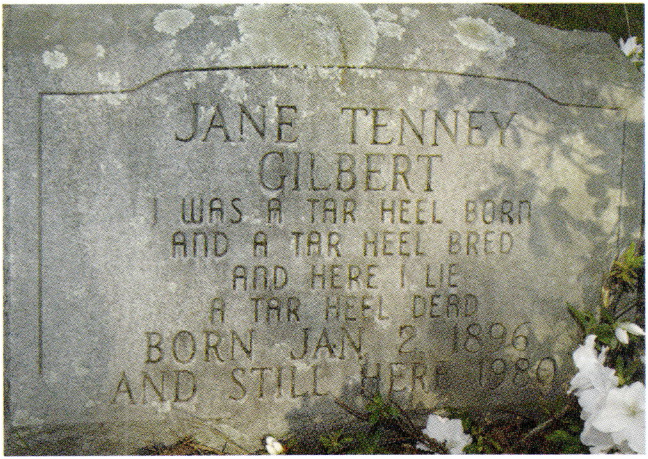

Jane Tenney
Gilbert
I was a tar heel born
And a tar heel bred
And here I lie
A tar heel dead

Born Jan 2 1896
And still here 1980

Old Chapel Hill Cemetery, Orange County, North Carolina

("Tar heel" is a nickname for a native or resident of North Carolina, possibly from the tar that was once a major product of the state)

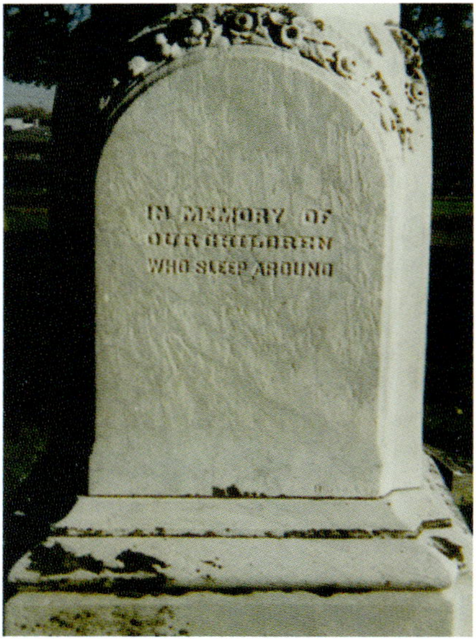

In memory of
Our children
Who sleep around

Richmond Cemetery, Richmond, Kentucky

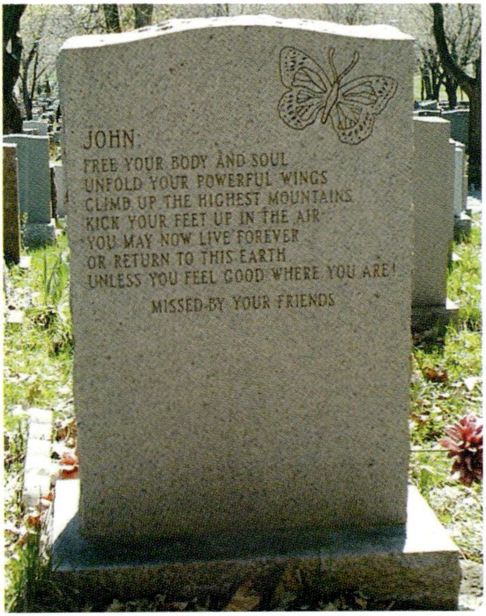

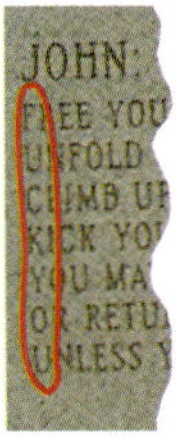

John
Free your body and soul
Unfold your powerful wings
Climb up the highest mountains
Kick your feet in the air
You may now live forever
Or return to this Earth
Unless you feel good where you are

Missed by your friends

Cimetière Notre-Dame-des-Neiges, Montreal

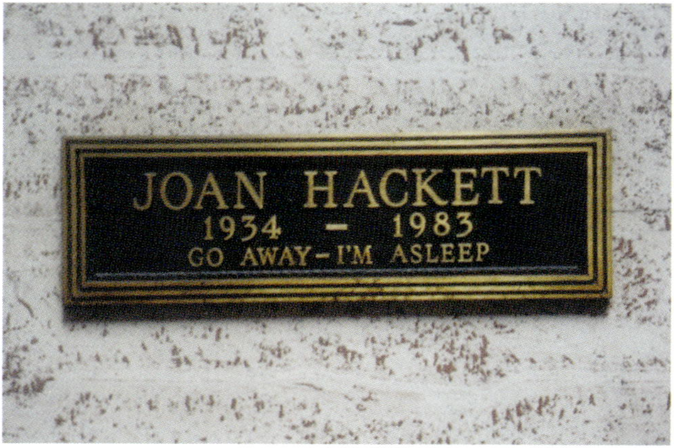

Joan Hackett
1934 – 1983

Go away – I'm asleep

Hollywood Forever, Hollywood, California

(Actress whose epitaph was taken from the sign she often hung on her dressing room door)

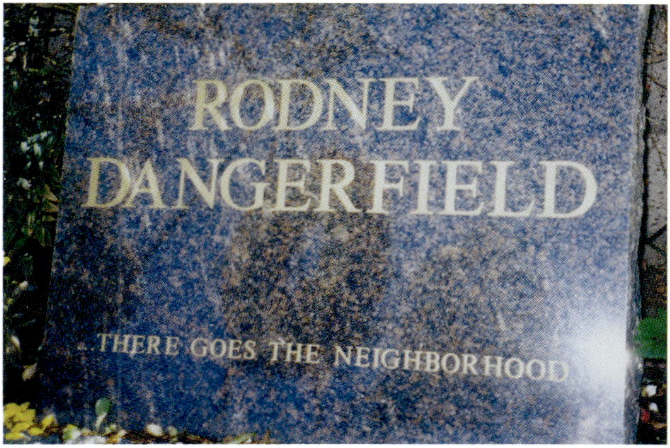

Rodney
Dangerfield

...There goes the neighborhood

Westwood Memorial Park, Los Angeles, California

(Popular comedian and master of the one-liner, known for his trademark "I don't get no respect")

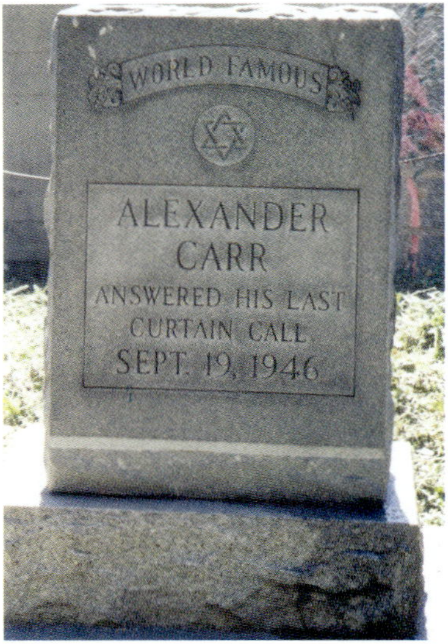

World famous

Alexander
Carr
Answered his last
Curtain call
Sept. 19, 1946

Hollywood Forever, Hollywood, California

(Russian-born actor who worked in the circus and theater before moving to Hollywood and appearing in silent films)

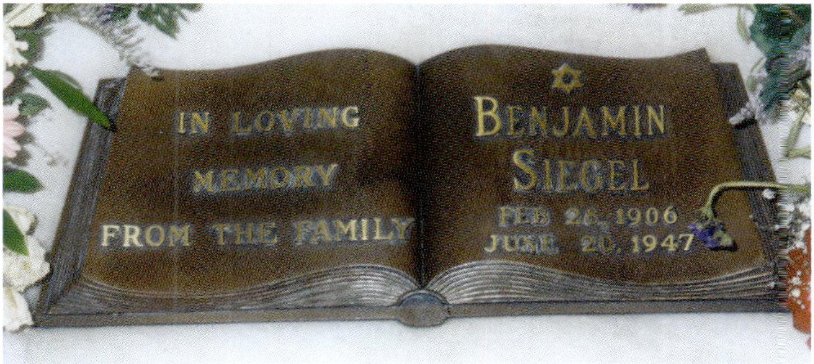

In loving
Memory
From the family

Benjamin Siegel
Feb 28, 1906
June 20, 1947

Hollywood Forever, Hollywood, California

(Famous gangster otherwise known as "Bugsy" Siegel)

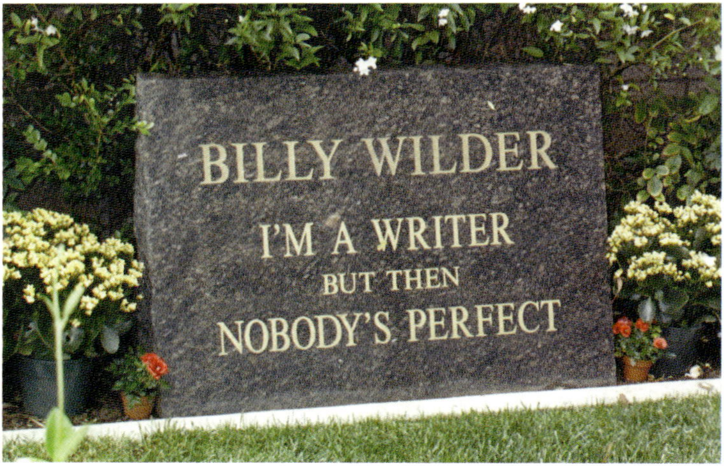

Billy Wilder

I'm a writer
But then
Nobody's perfect

Westwood Memorial Park, Los Angeles, California

(Celebrated screenwriter, director and producer; "Nobody's perfect" is the famous line from the end of his classic film *Some Like it Hot*)

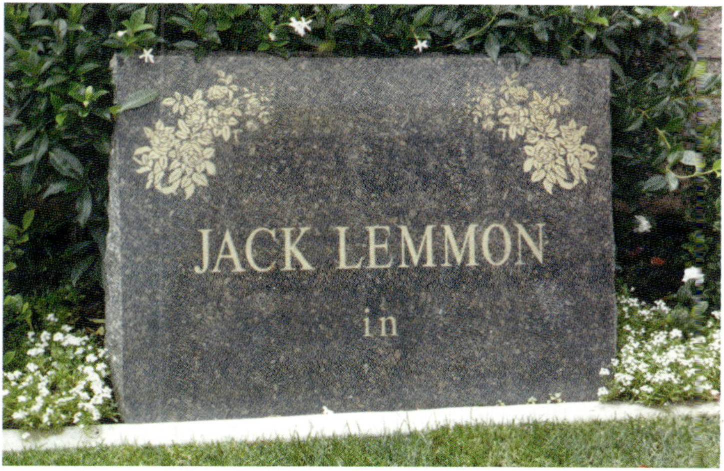

Jack Lemmon
in

Westwood Memorial Park, Los Angeles, California

(Oscar-winning actor whose films included *Some Like it Hot*)

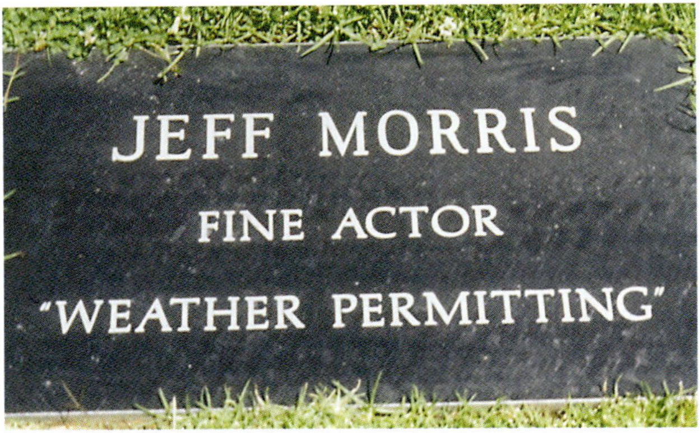

Jeff Morris

Fine actor
"Weather permitting"

Westwood Memorial Park, Los Angeles, California

(Texan film and tv actor who made several appearances in shows such as *Bonanza* and *Mission Impossible*)

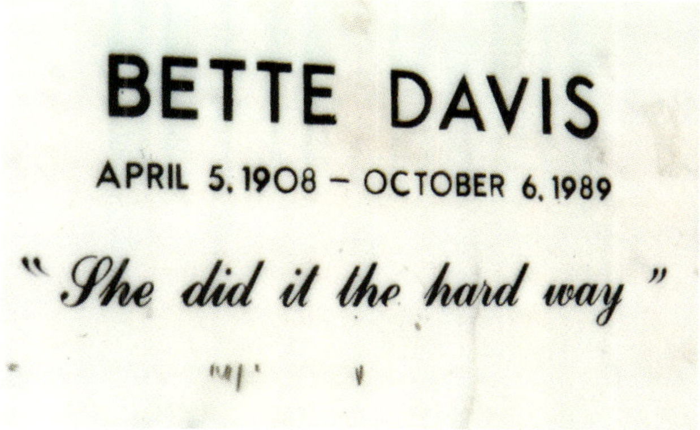

Bette Davies
April 5, 1908 – October 6, 1989

"She did it the hard way"

Forest Lawn, Hollywood Hills, California

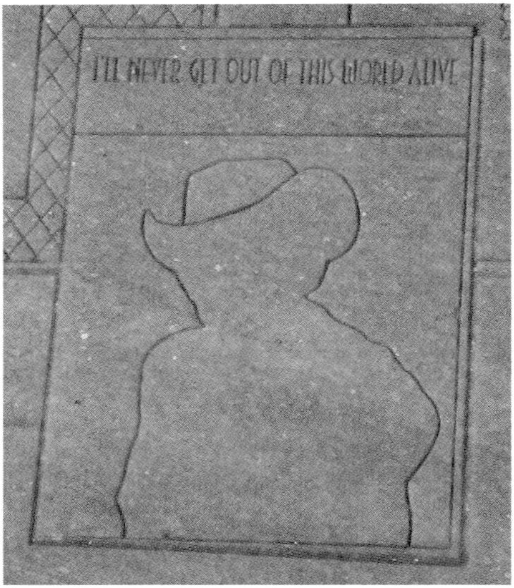

I'll never get out of this world alive

Oakwood Annex Cemetery, Montgomery, Alabama

(From the grave of Hank Williams (1923–1953), the legendary country singer; this is one of several song titles on his tombstone)

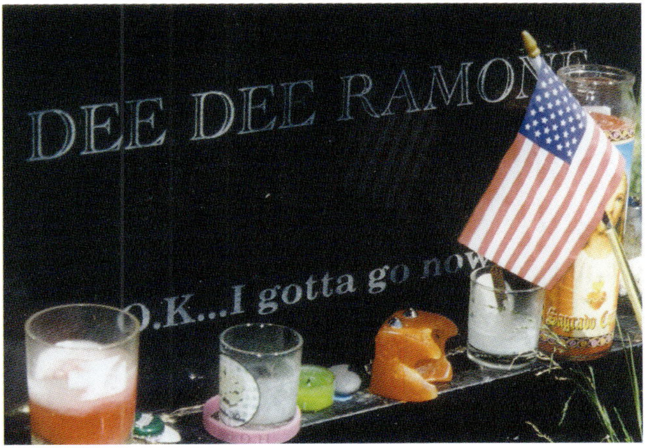

Dee Dee Ramone

O.K...I gotta go now

Hollywood Forever, Hollywood, California

(Dee Dee Ramone (1952–2002) was co-founder of the pioneering US punk rock band The Ramones, whose hits included *Let's Go*)

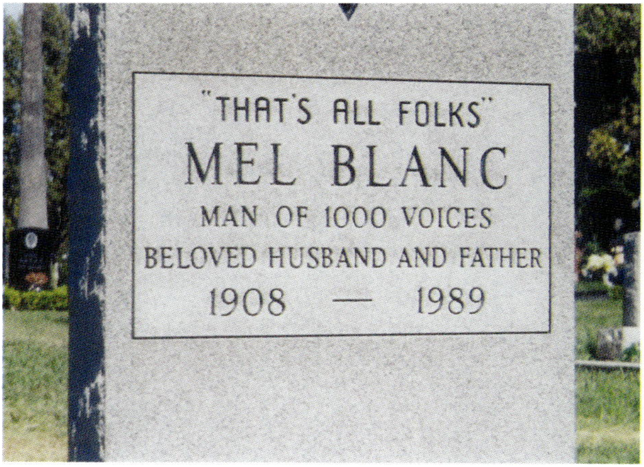

"That's all folks"

Mel Blanc
Man of 1000 voices
Beloved husband and father
1908 – 1989

Hollywood Forever, Hollywood, California

(Renowned voice actor whose repertoire included Bugs Bunny, Porky Pig, Yosemite Sam and Sylvester)

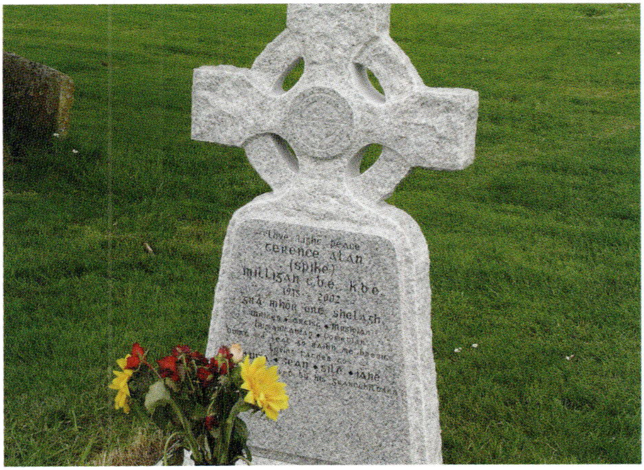

Love light peace
Terence Alan
(Spike)
Milligan c.b.e, k.b.e.
1918 – 2002
Gra mhor ort Shelagh
Writer ♦ Artist ♦ Musician
Humanitarian ♦ Comedian
Duirt me leat go raibh me breoite
Loving father to Laura ♦ Sean ♦ Sile ♦ Jane
Eternally loved by his grandchildren

St Thomas's Church, Winchelsea, East Sussex

(The Gaelic phrase *Duirt me leat go raibh me breoite* translates as "I told you I was ill")

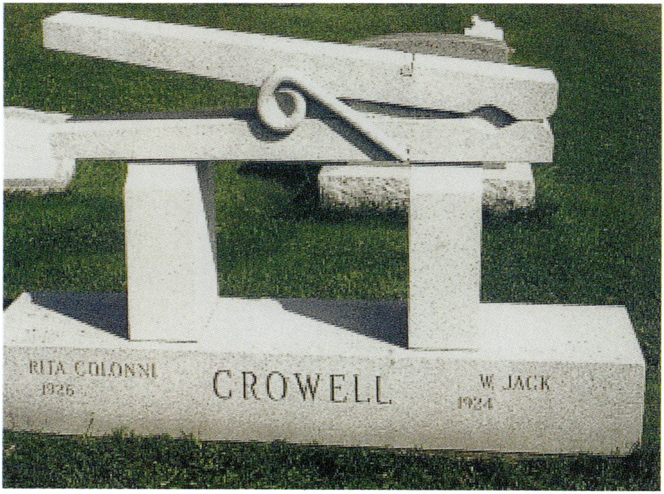

Rita Colonni Crowell W. Jack
1926 1924

Middlesex Cemetery, Vermont

(There are no death dates on this grave – it is a "pre-need" monument. The photographer tracked down Jack Crowell and asked him, "Why the clothespin?" To which he replied, "I own the company that makes them.")

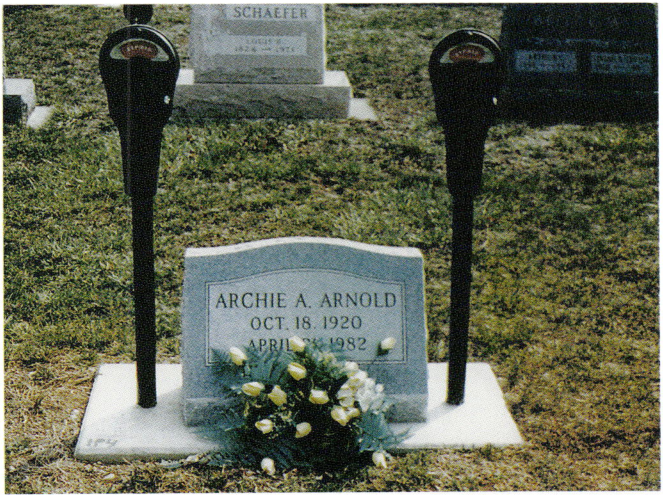

Archie A. Arnold
Oct. 18 1930
April 24 1982

Scippio Cemetery, Harlan, Indiana

(When the city of Hicksville, Ohio, removed all of its parking meters and sold them off, Archie Arnold, a local practical joker, bought two and took them to a funeral parlour to hold until his death; they are set on "Expired")

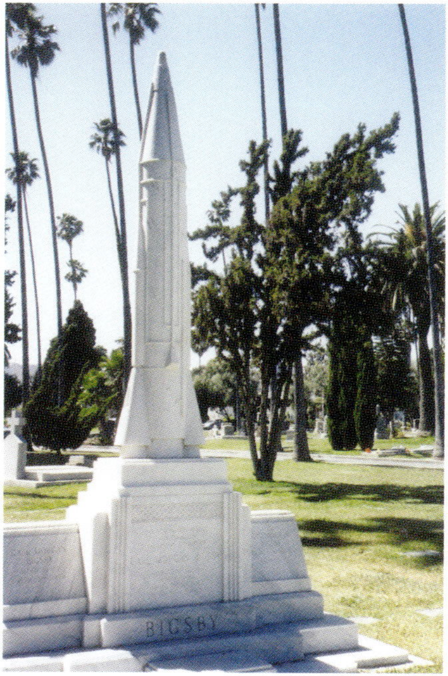

Carl Morgan
Bigsby

Retired by God
1898–1959

Constance W.
Bigsby

Too bad ... we had fun
1914–

Bigsby

Hollywood Forever, Hollywood, California

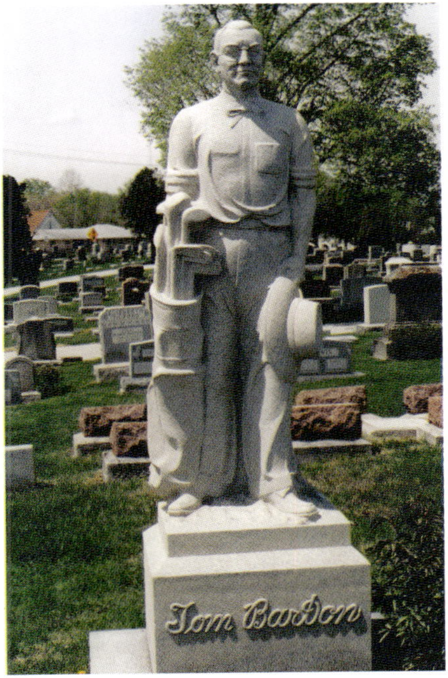

Tom Barton

Bedford Cemetery, Indiana

(Tom Barton was so obsessed with golf that upon his death, his family commissioned this carving of him)

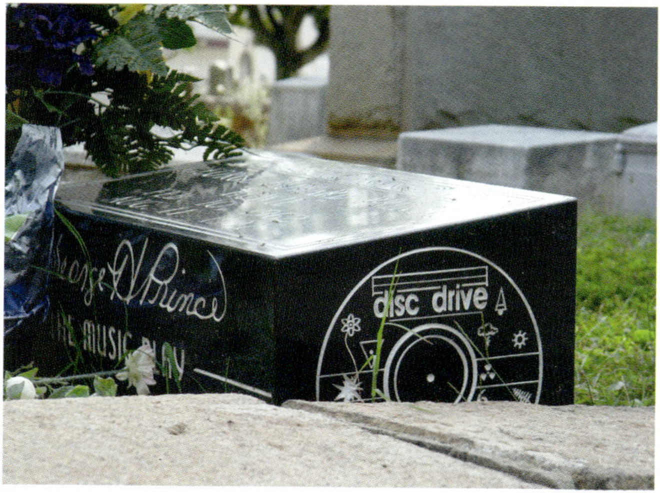

George H Prince

Let the music play

Disc drive

Oakland Cemetery, Atlanta, Georgia

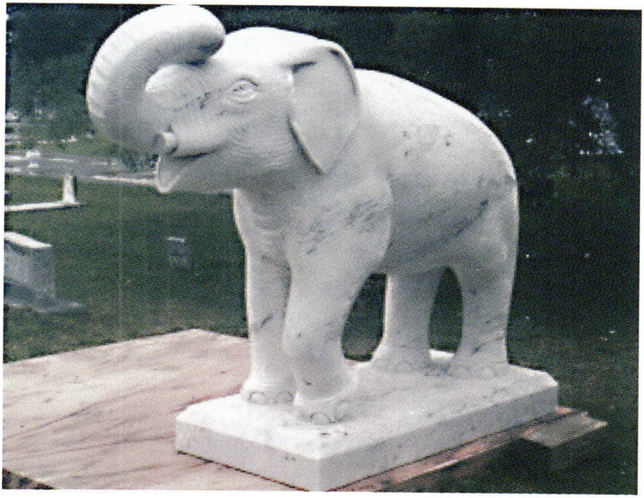

Moultree Cemetery, Moultree, Georgia

(The grave of a man who had a 3-ring circus and a pet baby elephant that followed him around with its trunk in his pocket, looking for peanuts; when the man died of a heart attack the circus employees took up a collection and had this marble statue carved over his grave)

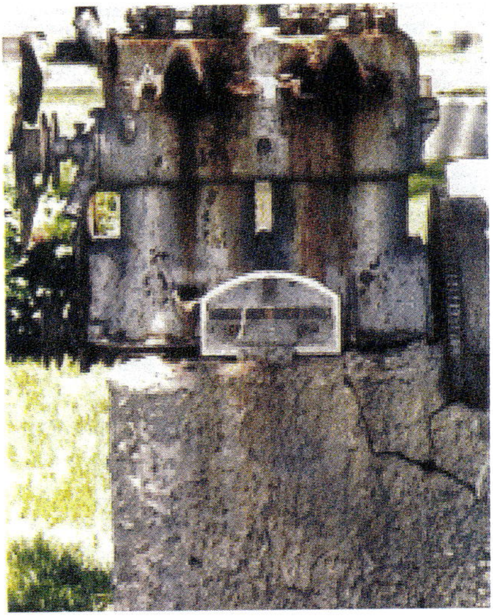

Cemetery at Garden City, Kansas

(The grave of a boy whose car crashed into a train during the Great Depression of 1929; his family couldn't afford a monument, so they mounted the engine from the car, a 1928 Chevrolet, on a cement block and placed an aluminium tag with his name, birth date and death date next to it)

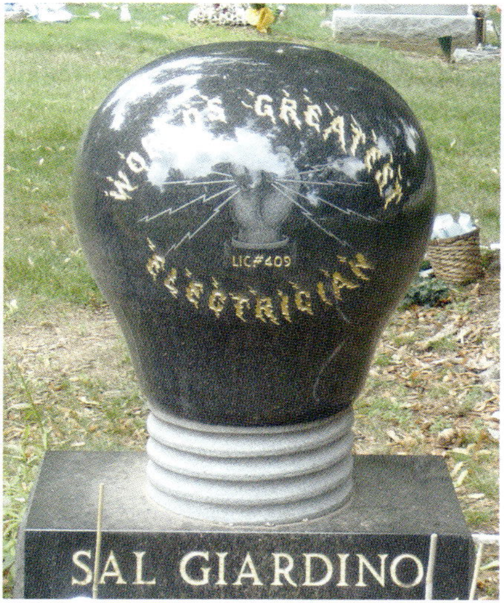

World's greatest electrician

Sal Giardino

Laurel Grove Cemetery, Totowa, New Jersey

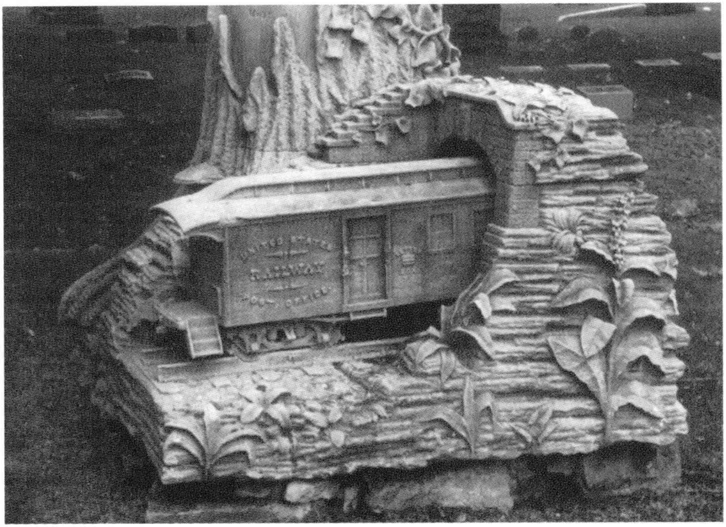

Rosehill Cemetery and Mausoleum, Chicago, Illinois

(The grave of George Bangs (dates of birth and death unknown), who invented the railroad mail car; this allowed the US Postal Service to sort mail as they travelled between cities, dropping off the mailbags at each station for local postal workers to distribute)

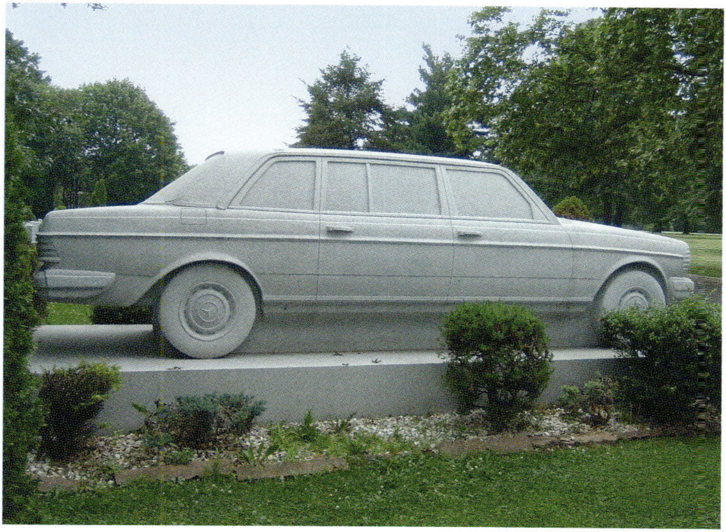

Rosedale and Rosehill Cemetery, Linden, New Jersey

(Raymond Tse died at the age of 15 and never had the chance to drive his dream car, a Mercedes-Benz, so his family had one carved for his grave; it weighs about 66 tons and was carved by 3 stone-cutters in amazing detail, with even a gas tank lid; the licence plates bear his name)

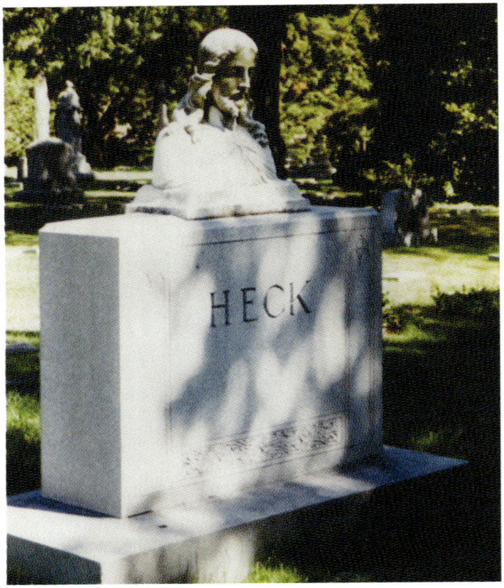

Heck

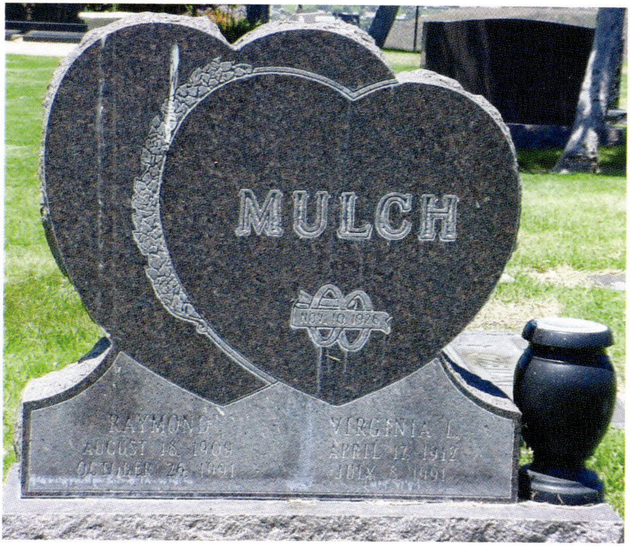
MULCH
NOV. 10, 1926
RAYMOND
AUGUST 16, 1909
VIRGINIA L.
APRIL 17, 1912

Mulch

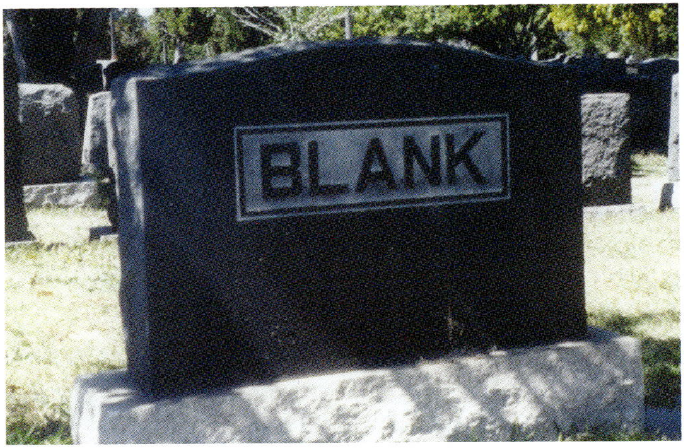

Blank

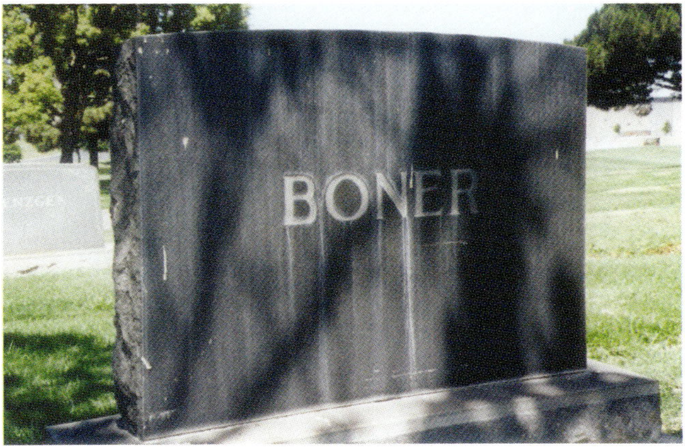

Boner

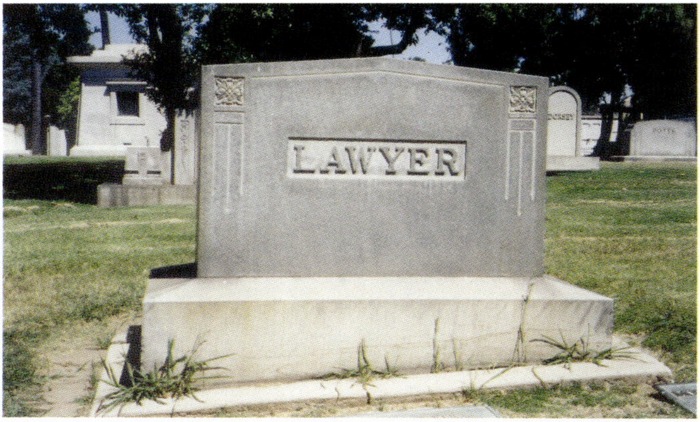

Lawyer

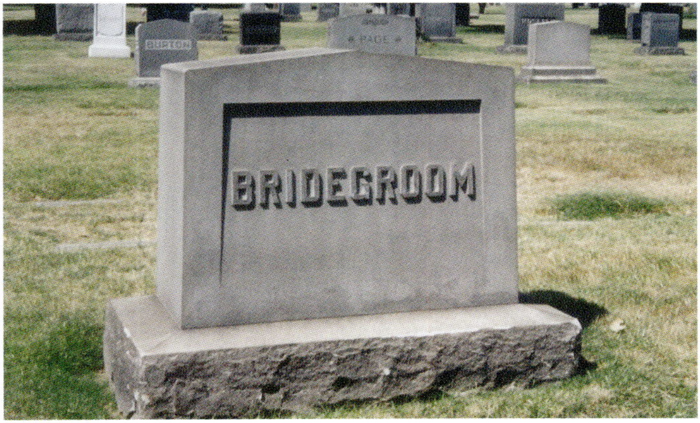

Bridegroom

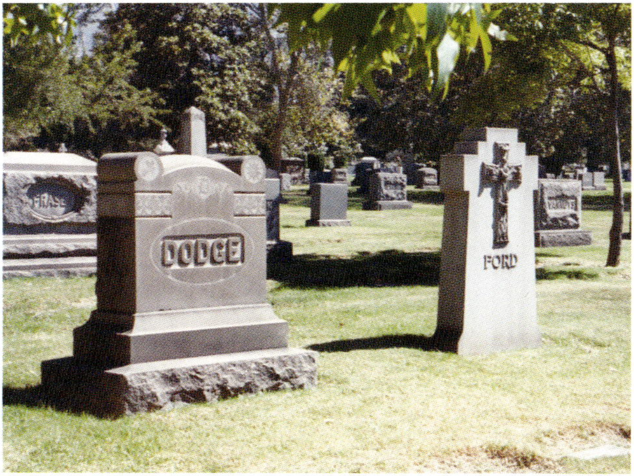

Dodge Ford

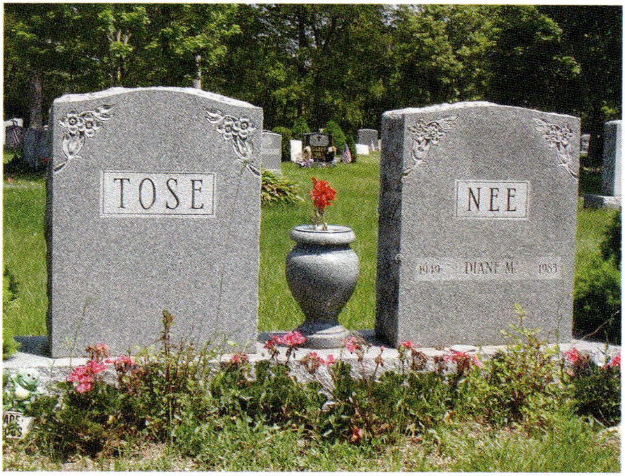

Tose Nee

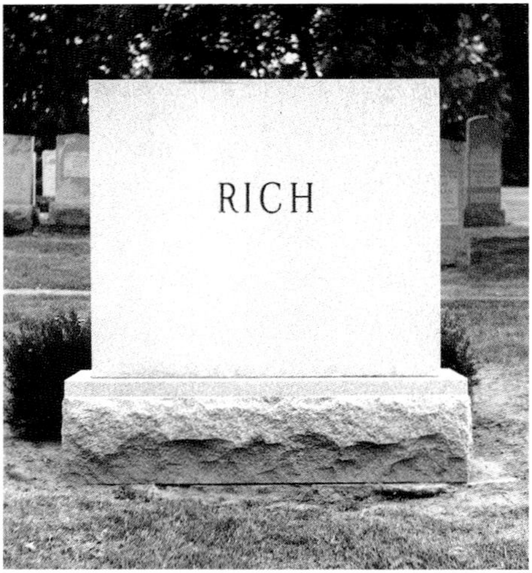

Rich

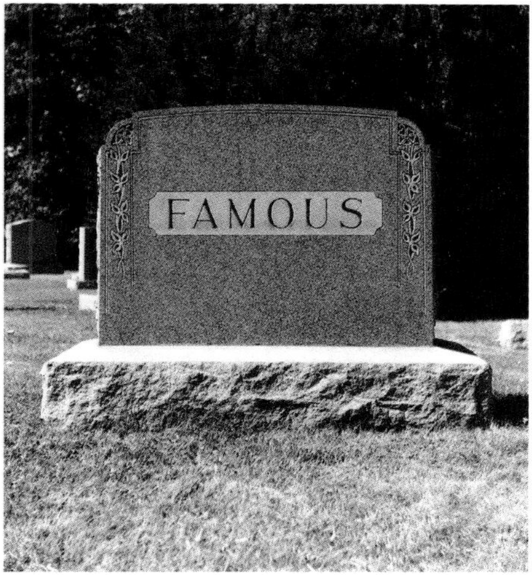

Famous

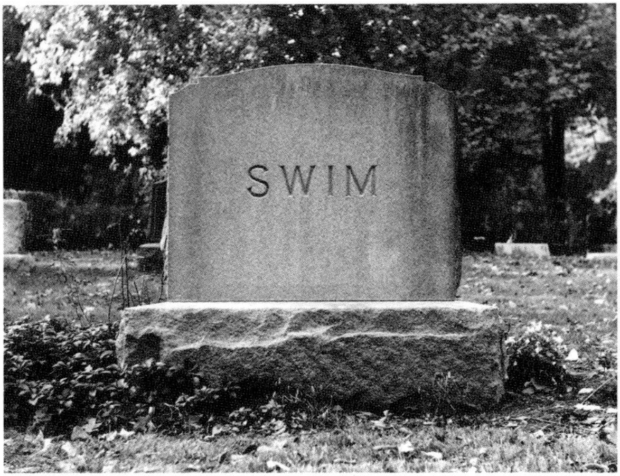

Swim

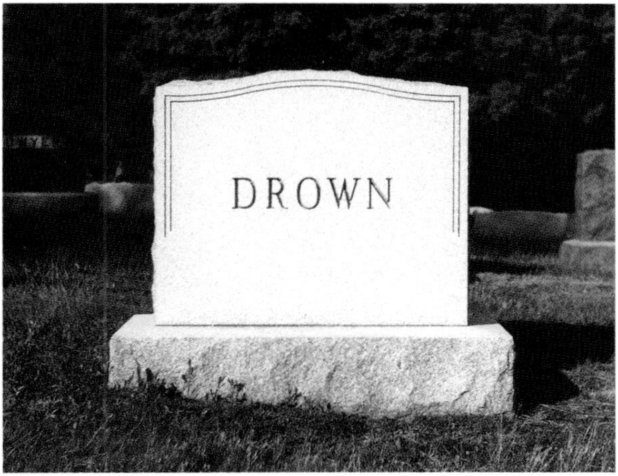

Drown

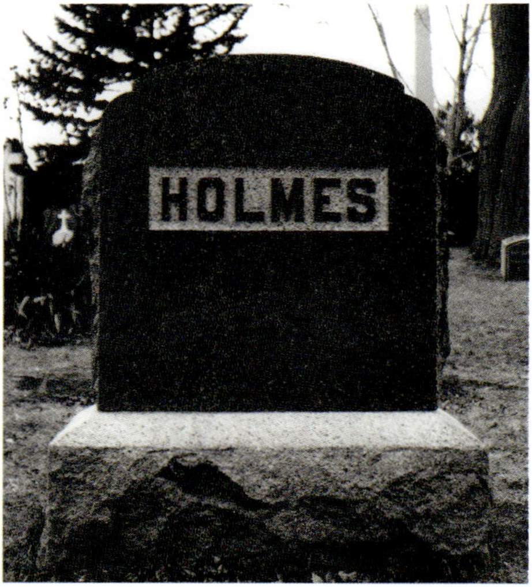

Holmes

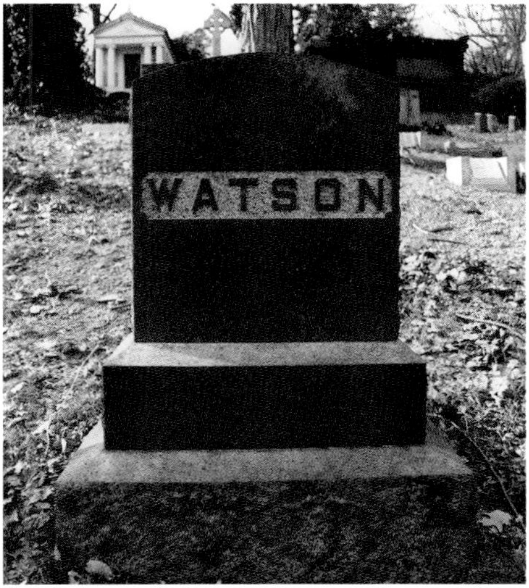

Watson

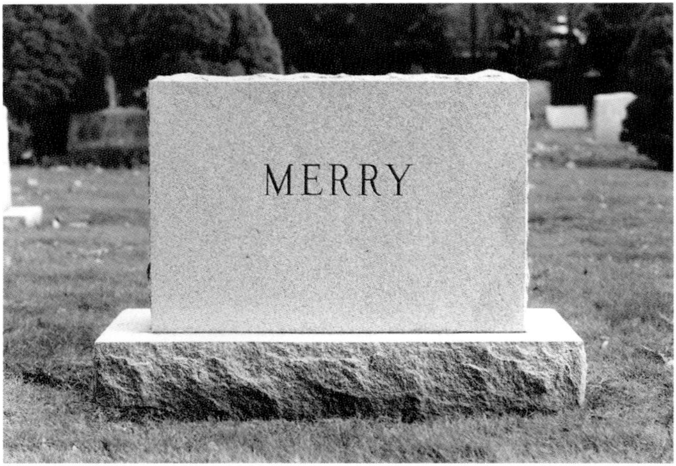

Merry

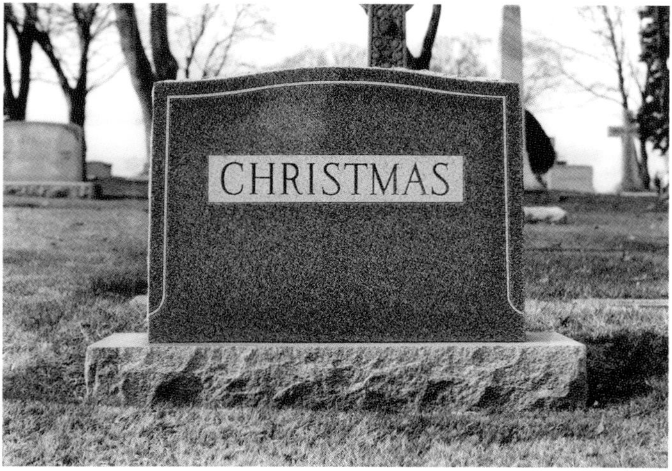

Christmas

Acknowledgements

We would like to thank the following for providing photographs for this book:

Beth Horsley/courtesy of Keven McQueen and Jo Blanset page 9
Clyde Chamberlin pages 34, 35, 37, 39, 40, 42
Emily Gray page 21
Gerry Glenister/www.glenister.info page 33
Kelly Jo Garner/www.hungryphotographer.org pages 14, 19
Keven McQueen and Jo Blanset pages 6, 7, 8, 12, 13, 15, 18, 20, 44
Richard A. Cooke/CORBIS page 17
Richard Argent pages 10, 11
Robert Zott/www.tombstoneguy.com pages 52, 53, 54, 55, 56, 57, 58, 59
Ryan Stowinsky/stuofdoom.com pages 41, 43
Steve Goldstein/www.beneathlosangeles.com pages 3, 22, 23, 24, 25, 26, 27, 28, 29, 31, 32, 36, 45, 46, 47, 48, 49, 50
Tad Merrick/courtesy of Keven McQueen and Jo Blanset page 15
Yves Poirier page 51
Zeny Williams/www.beyondthepalace.com pages 30, 38

The publisher has made every reasonable effort to contact all copyright holders. Any errors that may have occurred are inadvertent and anyone who for any reason has not been contacted is invited to write to the publisher so that full acknowledgement may be made in subsequent editions of this work.

First published in Great Britain in 2005
by Marlin Press
PO Box 8076
Stansted CM24 8XQ

2 4 6 8 10 9 7 5 3 1

ISBN 0-9547988-2-1

A catalogue record for this book is available from the British Library

Printed and bound in Singapore